About the Author .....
Introduction 7
Free bonus materials & printable resources 7
About the Book.. 8
The Needs Focused Approach 9
Active Learning Strategy #1 12
Mini Reviews 12
Active Learning Strategy #2 16
Teach-Backs 16
Active Learning Strategy #3 21
Student Involvers 21
Active Learning Strategy #4 29
Pair Work 29
Active Learning Strategy #5 34
Cooperative Group Work 34
Grouping Students for Cooperative & Active Learning 59
Grouping Methods 59
Diverse Groups 67
Managing Active Group Work Sessions 72
Managing Noise Levels During Active Sessions 79
Ten Extra Tips For Successful Group Work Sessions 81
And Finally! 83
Take Control of The Noisy Class 83

Review Request *86*
Suggested resource providers *88*
Strategies List *102*

"I used these ideas in class and had a wonderful day with my students."

Thank you so much!! I used these ideas in class and had a wonderful day with my students. As a first Year Relief Teacher I find this site invaluable in helping me become a better and more confident Teacher.

Jess (Take Control of the Noisy Class customer)

* * *

"It is very rewarding to see a teacher apply strategies from Rob's materials, then get excited as they see the 'magic' work."

"The materials have been right on target, students have benefitted as well as teachers. It is very rewarding to see a teacher apply strategies from Rob's materials, then get excited as they see the 'magic' work. Thank you for making my job easier and validating the experience."

Cheryl E. Le Fon (Take Control of the Noisy Class customer)

The Active Learning Tool kit

Outrageously Engaging Activities to Increase Participation, Raise Achievement & Have Your Toughest Students Asking for More

Needs-Focused Teaching Resource Book 3

Rob Plevin

http://www.needsfocusedteaching.com

Copyright 2017 Rob Plevin Needs Focused Teaching. Life Raft Media Ltd

ALL RIGHTS RESERVED.

The information in this document is protected by one or more world

wide copyright treaties and may not be reprinted, copied, redistributed, retransmitted,

photocopied, displayed, or stored electronically or by any means whatsoever without the express

written permission of the author.

DISCLAIMER AND/OR LEGAL NOTICES:

The information presented herein represents the view of the author as of the date of publication.

The author reserves the right to alter and update his opinion. This report is for information purposes only. It is not intended to provide exact or precise advice. The contents reflect the author's views acquired through his experience and knowledge on the subject under discussion. The author and publisher disclaim any liability for personal or business loss caused by the use of or misuse of or inability to use any or all of the information contained in this report. This report is a guide only, as such, use the information at your own risk.

About the Author

Rob Plevin is an ex-deputy head teacher and Special Education Teacher with the practical experience to help teachers in today's toughest classrooms.

No stranger to behaviour management issues, Rob was 'asked to leave' school as a teenager. Despite his rocky route through the education system he managed to follow his dream of becoming a teacher after spending several years working as an outdoor instructor, corporate trainer and youth worker for young people in crisis. Since then he has worked with challenging young people in residential settings, care units and tough schools and was most recently employed as Deputy Head at a PRU for children and teenagers with behaviour problems. He was identified as a key player in the team which turned the unit round from 'Special Measures'.

He now runs needsfocusedteaching.com, is the author of several books and presents training courses internationally for teachers, lecturers, parents and care workers on behaviour management & motivation. His live courses are frequently described as 'unforgettable' and he was rated as an 'outstanding' teacher by the UK's Office for Standards in Education.

Rob's courses and resources feature the Needs-Focused Approach™ – a very effective system for preventing and dealing with behaviour problems in which positive staff/student relationships are given highest priority.

To book Rob for INSET or to enquire about live training please visit the help desk at

www.needsfocusedteaching.com

Introduction

Free bonus materials & printable resources

This book, like the others in this series, is for teachers like you who want to connect and succeed with tough, hard-to-reach students in the shortest possible time. To help you do this, it comes complete with additional bonus material as well as printable resources to accompany the activities explained in the book.

Wherever you see the **'resource icon'** in this book, head over to our website to get your free resources and accompanying printables,

Please visit:

http://needsfocusedteaching.com/kindle/active/

About the Book

The Active Learning Tool Kit is book #3 in my Needs-Focused Teaching Resource series. This collection of teaching books is my attempt to provide teachers with practical, fast-acting, tried-and-tested strategies and resources that work like magic in today's toughest schools. The novel, quirky ideas and methods form part of my Needs Focused Approach and have been tried and tested with hard-to-reach, reluctant learners of all ages, in more than 40 countries. Over the last 10 years or more they have been found to be highly effective in improving learning, raising achievement, building trusting relationships and creating positive learning environments.

Each book in this series includes a comprehensive suite of bonus materials and printable resources as I want to give you as much support as possible and for you to be delighted with your book purchase. Please be sure to download your bonus resources from my website here:

http://needsfocusedteaching.com/kindle/active/

The Needs Focused Approach

The Needs-Focused Teaching System is explained fully in my main classroom management book, 'Take Control of the Noisy Class – From Chaos to Calm in 15 seconds'. It's available on Amazon in both Kindle and physical formats.

Briefly, this approach is based on Abraham Maslow's Hierarchy of Needs theory which suggests that human beings share a wide range of emotional and psychological needs – from the need to achieve through the need to contribute, to the need for love and a whole host of others in between.

By meeting these needs in the classroom teachers can effectively maximise student engagement while preventing behaviour problems which often arise due to feelings of boredom, frustration and alienation. We focus on just three broad groups - 'Empowerment' which includes things like recognition, freedom, autonomy, achievement, contribution, choice and competence; 'Fun' which includes curiosity, interest, growth and learning, adventure, amusement, surprise, variety; and finally the need to 'Belong' – to be accepted, valued, appreciated, needed, related to or connected with something beyond oneself.

If you think about it, few of us function well without adequate control, choice, autonomy and freedom in our lives - we need to be empowered. We can't live happy lives without at least some variety, humour, activity or fun. And we feel isolated and alone if we're not valued or appreciated by others or connected to them in some way - we need to belong. When these three needs are NOT being met - when they are missing from our lives - we tend to feel frustrated and unsettled. That's when the problems start.

Our psychological needs are crucial to us and must be satisfied – they are a primeval, subconscious thirst which must be quenched and as important to us as water and sunlight are to a plant. If the teacher doesn't provide a means to meet these needs as part of regular day-to-day practice, students will seek satisfaction in less appropriate ways of their own devising. In other words, if you don't give them fun, they'll make their own. If you don't give them a sense of power, they will assert themselves in their own way. And if you don't make them feel valued they will likely opt out and form trouble-making splinter groups.

The active and cooperative learning activities in this book will help students feel a sense of belonging – by making them feel part of the classroom community, by strengthening peer relationships and by building positive, mutually respectful student-teacher bonds. They will empower your students by providing them with realistic chances to achieve and experience success, by giving them a degree of autonomy and choice and by ensuring their efforts are recognised and acknowledged. And they will improve motivation in lessons by making lessons more interactive and appealing, more stimulating, more relevant and more fun.

The ideas and activities can be used for virtually any lesson topic or subject area to enliven the subject and deepen learning and retention through interaction and kinesthetic learning.

Let's make a quick start by looking at the benefits and some of the reasons why properly-managed active and cooperative group work sessions are so useful in today's classrooms...

Benefits of active and cooperative learning

1. There is less incentive for students to disrupt the lesson to get your attention because attention is being received naturally - from learning partners or other members of the group.

2. Positive peer relationships are developed. As a result of students helping each other to reach a common goal, they build strong bonds. And this helps build a sense of community in class.

3. Lower achieving students gain confidence and motivation. By working collaboratively with higher achieving students, low achieving students are able to take part in activities without feeling they lack necessary skills and understanding. By being actively involved in the lesson activities (instead of being bored or frustrated) they are less prone to disrupt. The high ability students also benefit through the process of guiding and supporting their fellow group members - their understanding of the material is reinforced.

4. Social skills are naturally developed. Skills such as self-expression, decision-making, responsibility, accountability, sharing, listening, conflict management are naturally practiced and developed during group work sessions. This has a knock-on effect of reducing the occurrence of behaviour problems brought about due to a lack of these skills.

5. It saves you, the teacher, your most precious resource... time. In many cases, once your students are used to a particular framework or activity, they effectively teach themselves and you find yourself free from constant requests for attention and help. This means you can actually enjoy giving quality support when it is required rather than when it's demanded – a real win-win situation.

Now, without further ado, let's get started...

Active Learning Strategy #1

Mini Reviews

Mini Reviews can be used to inject some energy into the lesson at any stage. They are also a very effective way to reinforce any piece of learning. Students remember very little from a lesson if they only hear the information – possibly as little as 10%. When they are given chance to repeat it, this figure goes up dramatically. Aim to split teacher talk and theory sessions up with frequent Mini Reviews.

Mini Review #1

Active Reviews

Star Jumps

1. Ask the whole class to stand up and stand in the shape of a star (as in 'star jump' – legs apart, arms apart reaching upwards).

2. Tell them they can't move until someone shouts out one topic-related important piece of information they've picked up from the lesson or previous lessons.

3. As soon as someone shouts something relevant, everyone jumps to the second phase of a star jump – legs together, hands down by sides.

4. Repeat the process until everyone has completed about ten jumps.

Joggers

1. Ask the whole class to stand up.

2. Ask a student to call out a number between one and twenty (or between one and ten – you'll see why it might be best to reduce this number in a moment). This is the 'Target Number'.

3. Tell students to start jogging on the spot.

4. Students have to continue jogging on the spot until sufficient (depending on the target number) relevant, topic-related facts have been called out.

Hops

1. Ask the whole class to stand up.

2. Ask a student to call out a number between one and twenty (or between one and ten – you'll see why it might be best to reduce this number in a moment). This is the 'Target Number'.

3. Tell students to start hopping on the spot.

4. Students have to continue hopping on the spot until sufficient (depending on the target number) relevant, topic-related facts have been called out.

Fireworks

Tell students that a 'firework' is when a student jumps up from their seat and contributes something positive to the lesson e.g. by stating what they've learned so far or stating how they plan to use the information they've learned. Start a timer and tell students you need to see fifteen 'fireworks' in the next 60 seconds. Sometimes an incentive may be helpful...

"OK, it's break time in ten minutes but if you want your break I need to see fifteen fireworks in the next sixty seconds."

Mini Review #2

Reflective Reviews

It's good to alter teaching styles so that one particular style doesn't become stale. Here are some calm, reflective-type reviews to slip in between the more active, fast-paced reviews above to vary the pace of the lesson...

"Write one sentence explaining what you just learned."

"Draw a quick sketch to help you remember what you just learned."

"Write three short sentences about the last twenty minutes and highlight the most important one."

"Write the words 'I will remember this bit' next to three pieces of information on your page."

Mini Review #3

Paired Reviews

Split the class into learning partners and identify each partner as either 'A' or 'B'.

Paired Review 1:

"Partner 'A', turn to your partner and tell him/her three things you learned in the last thirty minutes."

"Partner 'A', turn to your partner and ask him/her a question about the last piece of information to see how much they have learned."

"Partner 'A', turn to your partner and give him/her, in your own words, a summary of what we've just learned."

(Swap these roles during the next Paired Review so that B turns to A and does the talking.)

Mini Review #4

Picture Reviews

"Draw a symbol, shape, cartoon or squiggle to represent what you've just learned. Show your partner and explain it to them."

"Write six key words from the information we've just covered. Draw a picture/shape/cartoon/symbol/doodle to represent each word."

Active Learning Strategy #2

Teach-Backs

Teach-back activities are fun ways to encourage students to cement their learning by teaching others what they have been taught – by demonstrating, explaining and... er...teaching. Remember the saying 'You never really learn anything until you teach it'?

But as well as helping students learn new information, Teach-Backs are great for the teacher too because they let you check for understanding and see how much your students have learned. They also give you a bit of free time for a snooze. (Only joking)

Teach-Back #1

Ready, Steady... TEACH!

No materials required. This is a ritual or routine to build up with your students which can be used as a quick, (often extremely lively), review at the end of any phase of teacher-talk or explanation.

It is as effective as it is simple.

You explain to your students that whenever you call out the words (in your best Ainsley Harriet voice) "Ready, Steady... TEACH!", they are to work with their allotted learning partner for thirty seconds to a minute to Teach-Back what they have learned moments before.

Learning partners should be numbered one and two because this Teach-Back has three phases.

Phase one: After teaching the group the new information the teacher asks if there are any questions before moving on in order to clarify the learning and eliminate misunderstandings during the next stage.

Phase two: The teacher calls "Ready, Steady... TEACH!" and partner one immediately starts teaching partner two the new concept. It is important that they are encouraged to over-emphasise the key points with facial expressions and big hand gestures – humour makes learning stick – and that they move through the information quickly. For a difficult concept students are given up to a minute to teach back the key points of the new information but it is best to keep the activity brief – once partners lose interest, the effect is lost. This has to be a fast-paced brief review – nothing more.

Phase three: The teacher calls 'Come in Number one, your time is up' (or something similar) to bring the first session of teaching to a close and partners swap roles. On the second call of "Ready, Steady... TEACH!", partner two teaches partner one.

Partners then thank each other for being wonderful teachers and then the lesson continues.

Teach-Back #2

Group Teach-Back

In this version, table groups are given a specific piece of content to Teach-Back to the whole class.

For simple reviews each group is given five minutes to prepare a short presentation of up to three minutes. To keep presentations brief (difficult to do with groups), and add some mirth to the proceedings, students are only allowed to stand on one leg while speaking.

For presentations where groups are encouraged to use visual aids such as slides, charts and posters or demonstrations involving equipment more time is allocated.

Table groups make their presentations to the whole class.

Teach-back #3

Case Studies

In this teach-back students work in groups to create their own case studies focusing on handling difficulties and in a certain, given situation. The first few times you use this activity students will benefit from being given sample case studies as examples. The idea is that each group will create a case study which can then be presented to other groups for discussion.

1. Explain to students that the purpose of a case study is to learn about a topic by examining a concrete situation that reflects the topic. Show them some examples of case studies. Case studies can be a description of a situation or an excerpt of dialogue from a situation such as the one below from one of our Classroom Management courses:

2. Give students guidelines for completion of the case studies:

- Case study can be either real or invented

- Keep it fairly simple and within a given word limit

- Include two questions which you would like answering

Suggested questions for each case study include:

"What would you do in this situation?"

"How does this relate to ……?"

"If you were (the victim/shop-keeper/student/etc.) what would you do?"

"What five mistakes did the person make in this situation?"

"What five things did the person do right in this situation?"

"Give three examples of… from the above case study"

Teach-back #4

Posters

1. Students work in pairs or in groups of three or four.

2. Each pair/group must produce a quick poster explaining the topic area.

3. Coloured pens and poster materials are provided for each group.

Tip 1: Give each group member a different coloured pen so you can see that all students have contributed to the poster.

Tip 2: Give students a limit on the number of words used on their poster. Tell them they can use symbols and pictures but only a maximum of ten words. If you don't do this, some posters will be little more than an essay or series of numbered sentences in different colours with little thought going into the teaching behind those sentences.

4. Pairs/groups complete the posters and present back to the rest of the class.

5. Posters are displayed on walls and used as a starting point for next lesson.

Teach-back #5

Random Teach-back

1. Five summary questions are written on the board/white board relevant to the preceding teacher-talk/theory segment. (Teacher prepares these in advance of the lesson).

2. A question is selected from the list and all students are given thirty seconds to prepare their own answer. (At this stage nobody knows who will be chosen to do the teach-back so all students prepare an answer in case they are chosen).

 The Random Name Generator from your resource area is then used to select a student to do a Random Teach-back. Get your resources here:

http://needsfocusedteaching.com/kindle/active/)

3. The chosen student is given thirty seconds to answer the question by teaching back to the class using exaggerated hand gestures, facial expressions, dramatic voices etc.

Active Learning Strategy #3

Student Involvers

The following ideas are aimed at involving students in the teaching and learning process.

Whenever you actively involve students you will:

- Hold their attention and interest in the subject

- Improve retention rates

- Deepen learning and comprehension

- Keep them awake

Years ago I saw the stage version of 'Whose Line Is It Anyway', the popular improvisation comedy show. For the first half of the show the cast did their thing, and we in the audience did ours, happy to sit back and be entertained. And then one of the performers turned to us and said, with wicked grin, "And now it's your turn..." If he'd wired us up to the electricity grid he couldn't have charged the atmosphere faster. From that point on, we weren't audience, we were all part of the show. This was active involvement in action!

'Active involvement' takes the teaching process one step further by removing the invisible line between teacher and students. The following ideas are designed to help you get your students to become active participants in their own education.

Student Involver #1

FOCUS CARDS

This first activity is particularly useful during lengthy, didactic teacher-talk/lecture sessions.

1. Give each student several (say five or six) index cards on entry to the room, or split students into groups and give each group a pile of cards in the centre of the table.

At the start of the teacher-talk session the teacher gives the following instruction:

"Take one of your index cards and write down three things you want to learn about this lesson (topic). Put a big 'number 1' at the top of the card and then put it on one side."

Give the students a few minutes to complete these cards.

2. About ten minutes into the session, once the first concept has been covered, give students the following instruction:

"Take another card from the pile and write down a simple quiz question based on what we've just covered. (Suitable questions could be suggested for low ability students). Put a big 'number 2' at the top of this card and pass it to the person to the right of you - but don't read the new card you receive just yet."

Give students time to write and pass their cards. Once they receive a new card (someone else's 'number 2' card) they write an answer under the question, sign it, and pass this card along the line. Each person should now have a 'number 2' card with a quiz question and an answer.

3. The process is repeated after each new key concept has been covered so that students build up two, three or four (or even more) cards in addition to their 'number 1' card with questions and answers on. At each stage of the session, key points are thus reviewed.

4. At the end of the session during the plenary, students are asked to read out the answers on the cards they have accrued for each of the key concepts, together with the statements they wrote on their 'number 1' card. Answers are discussed as a group.

Variations:

Instead of writing quiz questions, students could:

- Compare their past knowledge about the concept with new knowledge.

- Write down how they would apply this new knowledge to a practical activity or real-life situation.

- Write a TRUE/FALSE statement – the student who receives the card indicates whether they feel the statement is true or false.

Student Involver #2

MANTRAS

Mantras are a fun way to gradually build up key points in students' minds through the simplest of all learning strategies – repetition. This is a method I learned from psychologist Rob Long and I use it regularly in our training courses and live workshops on working with challenging students - each short section is summed up with a simple but easily remembered 'mantra'.

The mantra is nothing more than a sentence which sums up the relevant key concept - but it gives an opportunity to cement ten or fifteen minutes' worth of information into a few words which can be repeated at any stage throughout the main lesson. By frequently requesting students to shout out the mantra in unison, the learning is cemented.

For example, after a section on changing negative attitudes when dealing with difficult students we introduce the mantra 'positive attitudes bring positive results' to emphasise and reiterate the importance of not jumping to negative assumptions when dealing with tough students.

At any stage of the session we might then shout:

"Ok, what have we learned?"

Positive attitudes...

...and after each part-finished sentence the audience or students complete the mantra.

You can build up the repertoire of mantras as the subject knowledge increases. Then to build on this foundation, going through the growing list of mantras as a group can become an effective starter, energiser or plenary activity which further cements the students' understanding of the subject.

Student Involver #3

FUN ROUTINES

We mentioned the power of routines as a classroom management tool in Managing Cooperative Group Work Sessions above and while they are incredibly useful as a classroom management tool, they don't always have to be authoritarian. They can be used effectively to add interaction to the lesson in a fun way.

One of the easiest ways to get student involvement is simply to ask for it; and as you read the ideas in this section you'll realise that there really is no limit to the fun routines you can build up in your teaching. The more regular, frequent interaction you build into your lessons in this way, the more fun your lessons will be – for both you and your students. It would be impossible to write suggestions which will appeal to everyone as we all have our individual styles, but hopefully the following ideas will serve as useful starting points for you to develop your own fun routines.

I used a very simple version of this technique when I worked as a corporate trainer. The company I worked for ran courses on leadership and motivation using very 'gung-ho' activities like off-road driving, paragliding, abseiling and paintball; the emphasis was on adrenalin and fun. The basic principle of interacting with trainees at every opportunity – getting them to repeat instructions (often in a silly voice) and celebrate even the tiniest successes in over-the-top ways was common.

Once I started teaching I found the same motivational/interactive ideas worked tremendously in the classroom and later came across a website called Power Teaching (now called 'Whole Brain Teaching') which has some amazing ideas and resources (all for free) on this topic. Chris Biffle who runs Whole Brain Teaching produces a huge range of free resources to help teachers develop this very interactive and fun style of teaching at his website: www.wholebrainteaching.com

The following fun routines are our own versions of those found on the Whole Brain Teaching website plus a couple of my own from my teaching days thrown in for good measure. Use these as a starting point and aim to develop your own using your own style and personality...

Fun Routine #1

Okay!

You: Whenever I say 'okay' to you all I need you to respond with 'okay sir' so that I know you're following me. Okay?

Them: Okay sir.

You: That's the ticket. But now let's make it a bit more fun – you must also respond in the same voice I use. [squeaky] Okay?

Them: [squeaky*] Okay sir!

Fun Routine #2

Sir, Yes Sir!

(If you've seen the drill scenes in 'Full Metal Jacket' or 'An Officer and a Gentleman', you'll know exactly how this one works. You might also want to warn teachers in any adjoining classrooms about the impending increase in noise levels!).

You: Whenever I need you to listen really closely to me I'm going to say one word: 'atten-tion!'... and I want you all to respond by shouting 'sir yes sir!' [John Wayne drawl] Okay?

Them: Okay sir!

You: [Sergeant Major voice] Atteeeeeen-tion!

Them: Sir yes sir!!

What is important in these examples is getting the routine in place so that they respond when they are supposed to – this is what keeps them actively involved; the actual content of the words isn't as important. The more fun you can make this the better.

Similarly, we can use fun routines for other aspects of the lesson such as giving praise (see 'Golf Claps' below), making important announcements, emphasising particular pieces of information ('Are you listening') and keeping students motivated ('Yahoo/Yaboo'). With a little imagination there really is no limit to the fun you can inject into a lesson and the involvement you can generate.

Fun Routine #3

Golf Claps

You: Whenever someone does something which is worthy of applause I'll say 'golf clap' and we'll all give them a brief round of polite applause. [Demonstrate].

Definition:

A golf clap is performed by lightly tapping the fingertips of one hand against the palm of the other hand, thereby creating the effect of spectators clapping quietly & politely during a golf game. Although usually considered a form of sarcasm, delivered after a disastrous moment or embarrassing incident, a golf clap can be used as a light-hearted celebration when delivered with a smile.

Fun Routine #4

Are you listening?

You: When I'm about to make an important point I'm going to ask 'are you listening?' with my hands behind my ears, as though I'm an elephant. [Deep elephant voice] Okay?

Them: Okay sir!

You: And when I say that you respond by saying 'ready and waiting' with your elbows on the table and your finger pointing towards me. So, [elephant ears] are you listening?

Them: Ready and waiting.

You: Excellent. O-o-o-kay.

Them: O-o-o-kay!

Fun Routine #5

Yahoo/Yaboo

Here's one I use whenever a student gives a good answer, when I want to give some praise or when I want to bring the group's attention to something they've done wrong, such as noise levels getting too high.

You: Whenever I announce something good I'll put my hands in the air and smile (demonstrate a smile) and I want you all to yell 'yahoo!'. And when I announce something not so good I'll give you my miserable look (impersonate any of the cast of Eastenders) and you reply by moaning 'yaboo'. We'll try it out now... O-o-o-kay?

Them: O-o-o-kay!

You: There are only five minutes of the lesson left - .

Them: Yahoo!

You: Just long enough for me to set your homework - .

Them: Yaboo!

Active Learning Strategy #4

Pair Work

Here is a selection of tasks you can give to pairs of learning partners to increase participation in your lessons...

Pair Work Task #1

Peer Teach

Having explained or demonstrated a new concept to the class, have partners teach the main points to each other. It is most helpful to demonstrate EXCELLENT teaching first by making sure each partner understands the importance of CLARITY (sticking to 1-3 main points covered) and ENERGY (speaking with enthusiasm and passion). Peer teaching is a phenomenally powerful method for improving understanding – hence the saying 'you don't actually learn anything until you teach it'.

Keep sessions very brief, either to sum up lesson content, as a review activity or as a reminder to reinforce some difficult new information and always demonstrate and encourage appropriate, positive communication.

e.g.

i) 5 minutes: Partner one teaches; partner two listens

ii) Partner two thanks partner one and gives appropriate feedback (See below)

iii) 5 minutes: Partner two teaches; partner one listens and gives feedback

Appropriate feedback:

Thank you, I agree with...

I liked the way you explained...

I think you're very good at...

The best thing you brought up was...

Pair Work Task #2

Task Tennis

Have partners practice new skills by taking it in turns to complete a task and then 'pass' the activity over to their partner to first 'score' or assess and then try themselves. This framework can be adapted to use with any lesson topic. In order to make sure both partners are engaged, they should both be working on different tasks at the same time.

Pair Work Task #3

Test Each Other

Have partners test each other's knowledge on previous lesson content – either as a starter, review or mid-lesson activity.

Pair Work Task #4

Develop Questions

Get partners to devise and write questions to ask the rest of the group

Pair Work Task #5

Re-Cap

Get partners to re-cap part or all of the lesson by first summarising the key points and then feeding back to the group.

Pair Work Task #6

Reading to Each Other

Rather than have individuals read instructions, texts, directions etc. to themselves, get partners to read a section out to each other.

Grouping Students for Pair Work

Pairing Method #1

Find a Learning Partner

1. Students move round the room (music can be played if desired) and pair up either when directed by teacher or when the music stops.

2. When pairs have been formed, teacher asks a question or presents a task such as those below ('Six Tasks to Give Learning Partners')

3. Partners discuss the question/task for a predetermined time.

4. Process can be repeated with other pairings or students can feedback as a group.

Pairing Method #2

Hands Up (good for older students)

Students are counted off as you walk round the room assigning them either a number "one" or a number "two". (Try and ignore the guffaws relating to students labeled as 'number twos'!)

Number ones are then told to stand with their hands in the air until a number two pairs up with them.

This is a very quick and effective way of splitting partners who would normally sit next to each other and cause problems.

Pairing Method #3

Couples Cards

Couples Cards is a fun and easy way to randomly divide the class into pairs of students..

Materials: Index cards, one per student.

Directions:

1. Before the exercise begins, take the number of students you have in the class and divide it in half. If there is an odd number of

students in the class, divide the entire class in half, minus three students

2. Take the halved number of students, and come up with that many couples or different pairs, and write one half of the pair on each index card. For example, if you have 34 students in class, come up with 17 couples of pairs of objects, and write one half of the pair or couple on each one of the cards. These pairs must be easily recognizable to the students.

3. If the class has an odd number of students, for example 35, create 16 pairs or cards, plus one set of an easily identifiable triplicate. The pairs you come up with can be topic, pop culture, or society related, as long as students will easily be able to figure out their match.

4. Randomly hand out a card to each student in the class. Inform students that they are to read the word they have on their card, and find their match, in order to create a matching pair. Allow students to wander around the class until they have all found each other. If there is a set of three in the class, be sure to inform students of this beforehand so they will know to look for two matches to their card.

Sample Couples/Pairs:

Coffee and Donuts

Antony and Cleopatra

Milk and Cookies

Pen and Paper

Caesar and Brutus

Sample Triplicate:

Red, Blue, and Yellow (Primary colors)

Executive, Legislative, Judicial (Branches of Government)

Active Learning Strategy #5

Cooperative Group Work

The following activities are classed as both 'Cooperative' and 'active' in that they will get your students mixing and working together, and in doing so there will generally be an element of movement around the room.

Some of the activities are accompanied by a relevant printable resource sheet. You'll find these in your resource area here:

http://needsfocusedteaching.com/kindle/active/

I'll draw your attention to one of the resources right now to get you started – the 'Thank You, You Were Great' sheet. You can use this after any session of group work or partner work to show and teach students the value in appreciating each other. I've used sheets like this on our live courses and it is amazing how emotional some people get when they receive positive comments from others. The beauty of the sheet is that comments can be made without the fear of embarrassment which often comes with verbal appreciation.

Active/Cooperative Activity #1

Who Knows?

Number of people: Any group size

Materials: Teacher-prepared question cards or worksheets

Time: 20+ minutes depending on group size

Overview: A tremendous way for students to work as a group and share and discover knowledge

Directions:

1. Students start the activity in pairs and are given a sheet of 'Who Knows?' question cards

See Resource, here:

http://needsfocusedteaching.com/kindle/active/

2. Partner One asks partner two questions from his/her question sheet. Partner Two answers ONE question only and Partner One fills in their name on his/her sheet under the relevant question.

3. Partner Two checks and initials the question card and then asks Partner One a question from his/her sheet in the same way. Both partners thank each other appropriately.

4. On completion of this first round both partners then put one hand in the air to signal they are looking for a new partner. Once they have each found someone new, they repeat the two-way questioning, giving each other ONE answer each, before thanking each other and moving to a new partner.

5. Students repeat steps 1-4 until they have managed to get answers to all the questions on their sheets. Once they've completed their sheets, students sit down and complete a suitable 'early finisher' activity but

may be still approached by other students still working on their question sheets.

6. Students can either feedback as one group or can form sub-groups to discuss their answers before feeding back.

NOTE:

To use the 'Question Card' template simply type a separate suitable subject-based question in each box and photocopy one whole sheet for each student.

Active/Cooperative Activity #2

Group Learn & Teach

Overview: Aristotle said "teaching is the highest form of understanding" and most people in education agree – we understand something best when we actually teach it to someone else. This activity involves peer teaching and gives students the opportunity to act as both learners and teachers. It also frees the teacher from the teaching role allowing him/her to provide high-level support where necessary, or catch up on some sleep.

This is a very enjoyable and highly interactive way of teaching. Social skills - listening, engagement, and empathy - are also naturally developed through each member of the group having an essential part to play in the common goal. It can be used for a variety of information discovery/retrieval formats and any subject topic. As well as being an efficient means of teaching new material, this activity can also be used as an excellent end-of topic review.

Number of people: Any group size (minimum sixteen for groups of four, although smaller numbers can be accommodated by reducing the number in each group to three).

Materials: Research/background material sources in the form of videos, audio recordings, textbooks, reports, templates, results, guest speakers/topic experts etc.

Time: Whole lesson – allow 50 minutes minimum

Directions:

In an ideal world, for the activity to run smoothly, the whole group would be split into four groups of four students, i.e. there would only be sixteen learners in all. This would allow four topics to be taught/learned and is the optimum number as you will see below. We don't live in an ideal world (this one has politicians in it) and teachers have to cope with groups of up to forty-five in some cases and less than ten in others so we have to be creative and innovative. I will explain how the activity will run for sixteen learners and then show how, with some adaptation, the same activity can be successfully used with virtually any number of participants.

STAGE 1- Research (Suggested time, 15 minutes)

In this stage students are sent to their group area and given a subject to research/learn as a group. It is important to enforce a strict time limit to learn the material.

Each group is told to produce a 'Summative Poster' to explain the topic they are researching. (In practice, a wide range of tasks could be offered to the students. However, in this particular case the finished product is to be used as a crucial teaching aid during the second stage and so requires tight guidelines; the overall success depends on the quality of the finished result. For that reason, clear guidance as to completion is often required).

Having given this task many times I have learned to LIMIT the number of words used on the poster, otherwise the 'poster' quickly develops into an over-sized 'essay' with each participant wanting to add more and more information. It needs pointing out that each team's poster is to be used as a teaching aid during the next stage and its quality is therefore crucial to the smooth running of the activity. For that reason, it may be necessary to stifle creative flair with some groups and insist they stick to a relatively inflexible format.

My guidelines are as follows...

Task:

Produce a summative poster outlining up to ten key points about (topic). You can only use a maximum of ten words. You can use pictures/symbols but only ten words. You have 15 minutes to discuss, design and produce the poster.

STAGE 2 – Teaching and Learning (suggested time 10 minutes)

In this stage each group nominates a teammate who will act as 'teacher' during the next stage while the other members of the group go to be 'taught' by teachers from the other groups.

The 'teachers' stay in their own group area. It will be their job to teach their group's findings to a member of each of the other groups. The other three members of each group will assign themselves to a teacher from one of the other groups.

As shown in the diagram below, the green teacher will teach a member from each of the blue, red and yellow groups. A blue teacher will teach a member from each of the red, yellow and green groups, and so on.

Each learner is encouraged to take clear notes about the topic based on their teacher's summative poster and teaching.

STAGE 3 – Group Share (suggested time 15 minutes)

In this stage the original group members reform and learn from each other. Each of the three members who previously acted as 'learners' now act as teachers in their original groups and take turns to teach the information they received from the other groups' teachers to their original teammates.

There is no need for a review activity as such with this activity because each student has effectively both learned and taught the information – the review was built in.

Notes/variations:

There will rarely be exactly sixteen in your group. However, the activity can still be completed with far larger numbers by having multiple sub-groups within each main colour group, e.g. three sub-groups within each colour instead of one main colour group (three yellow groups of four, three green groups of four, three blue groups of four, and three red groups of four) would cater for forty-eight individuals. Where total numbers aren't divisible by four it is acceptable to have the odd group of five, and to have two individuals remain as teachers at stage two.

Active/Cooperative Activity #3

Pick a Card, Any Card

Overview: Students have individual roles within groups of three or four and play a card game to learn, cement or review information.

Number of people: Any group size

Materials: Pre-written question cards. You'll find these in your resources, here:

http://needsfocusedteaching.com/kindle/active/

Time: 15-30 min

Directions:

1. First student fans the cards with the questions facing him/her and says "Pick a card, any card!"

2. Second student picks a card and first reads it out loud. Second student answers the question without interruption from the rest of the group members.

3. Third student responds to second student's answer. This response can take several forms:

- If the answer is incorrect, the third student thanks the second student for his/her answer and then offers suggestions for improvement or explains the right answer. If necessary, help can be given from the first student but only when the third student has finished speaking.

- If the answer is correct the third student thanks and praises the second student and then paraphrases his/her answer.

Variations/notes:

The directions are written for groups of three although an extra role can be created by having the second student pick a card from the first student, then read the question out loud for the third student to answer while a fourth student takes the role of the third student above (responding to first student's answer).

Active/Cooperative Activity 4

First Aid

Overview: The main principle of this activity is to get students to work together to find their own solutions to their problems – from both a subject-based or personal perspective. It can be used as a basis for a whole lesson, as a fill-in activity, a starter or a plenary.

Number of people: Any group size. Students work in pairs.

Materials: 'Injury' and 'First Aid' cards. You'll find these in your resources, here:

http://needsfocusedteaching.com/kindle/active/

Time: Various, depending on situation – from 15 to 55 minutes

Directions:

1. Instruct students to write down on a scrap of paper something they would like clarifying or explaining – i.e. their subject 'injury'.

2. Pair up students into learning partners or hand out 'Injury' & 'First Aid' cards to randomly select pairs. (Each 'Injury' stands with one hand raised in the air until a 'First Aid' pairs up with them – both partners then sit down).

3. Each pair finds a space in the room and the 'Injury' reads out their problem or question relating to the topic. (Background music is useful at this stage to alleviate embarrassment of sharing information in public).

4. The 'First Aid' listens and then suggests solutions for the 'Injury'. The 'Injury' can write down the solutions offered if they are of use.

5. After 2-3 minutes, this stage is brought to a stop – either by turning off the background music or sounding a hooter. The 'First Aid' remains seated and the 'Injury' moves on to a new 'First Aid' for more solutions.

6. The process is repeated so that 'First Aid' is administered to 4 or 5 different 'Injuries'

before cards are swapped so that all students are given the opportunity to both offer

solutions and find answers to their questions in the same way.

Active/Cooperative Activity #5

Speed Dating

Overview: If you can get past the name this is a very useful activity which enables all students in a group to have brief contact with each other. The uses include offering feedback to each other, sharing views and ideas, swapping and comparing data, getting to know new members very quickly etc.

Number of people: Any group size.

Materials: A clip board for each student. A horn or buzzer to signify the end of each 'date' and a large timer on display. Templates and/or writing frames may be required for slow workers who may have difficulty recording information quickly.

Time: Various, depending on situation – from 15 to 55 minutes

Directions:

1. Explain the questions which are to be discussed/answered throughout the activity. A list of questions or suitable data could be provided for each student.

2. Arrange a line of tables with chairs opposite each other. Larger groups may require two or more lines of tables. An extra single chair is placed at the end of the line of tables. (Each person must take a turn in this 'Review chair' otherwise partners 'meet' each other too quickly so in the case of even numbers in the group, the teacher must also take part).

3. With students seated opposite each other across the tables, the hooter signifies the start of the activity and each pair has 3 minutes to share information. A second hooter signifies the end of the 'date' and each person moves 1 seat to their left to face a new partner.

4. The process is repeated until students meet up with their original partner.

Note:

Each cycle will mean a new person sitting in the 'Review chair' without a partner. This time is to be used to review their notes.

Active/Cooperative Activity #6

Carousel

Overview: Teams or pairs of students work through a variety of different activities in any order they choose. Activities vary in style but all relate to the same learning objective. Students benefit from the range of activities on offer catering for different learning styles and preferences as well as from being able to make their own choices in terms of the pace and order of their work.

Number of people: Any group size.

Materials: A range of learning stations with reference material, practical activities and demonstrations need to be set up such as:

- Audio and video sources - Watch/listen to the information and then answer the following questions...

- Reference books and text books - Use the information to produce a mind-map, newspaper report, advertisement, poster, summary, report etc.

- Internet access - Complete the following 'Online Scavenger Hunt' (see 'Engagement & Motivation')

- Practical equipment – set up the apparatus as shown in the diagram to find the solution to...

A large chart displayed on the wall with the learning stations listed in 1 column and space for students to sign their names in an adjacent column.

A clip board for each student with an individual copy of the learning stations chart – students sign both their own chart, as well as the class chart on completion of a task.

Time: At least one whole lesson needs to be allocated to this activity. If room constraints allow, there is scope to leave equipment set up and run the activity over two, three or four lessons.

Directions:

1. Students are presented with the challenge of completing a minimum number of activities within the allotted time (e.g. A minimum of six from the choice of 10) to allow slower workers to experience success while 'high flyers' still have opportunity to stretch themselves.

2. The teacher monitors groups as they undertake the tasks, (some input may be needed to prevent overcrowding at the more popular work stations for example) and provides support to those needing it.

3. When an activity has been completed, the group submit their work to the teacher for approval before being allowed to move to another activity.

Active/Cooperative Activity #7

The Round Table

Overview: The teacher gives students a task which promotes discussion and to which there are multiple answers. This format can be used for all kinds of activities such as problem solving, contributing written responses or adding information. This may take the form of adding suggestions to a list, as in a brain storming session; developing a diagram or plan; offering possible solutions to a question or contributing data from a research task etc.

Number of people: Any group size.

Materials: Paper and pens for each student or appropriate worksheet/project details

Time: This activity is very flexible. It can run for twenty minutes or an hour depending how much information you want students to produce.

Directions:

1. Students are placed in teams of four. Teams can be randomly selected but this activity works best with diverse groupings so that low ability students can be given the motivation and support they may need.

2. One student in each group is elected as leader and is responsible for starting the task. The leaders in each group write their contributions on a piece of paper or project sheet before passing it on to the next team member. In this way, each student gets to contribute to one project sheet.

Variation:

The method described above is ideal for brief contributions, where students only have to add a small amount of information such as a single idea or brief answer. Where students are required to give more information they can work simultaneously – each student working on their own task at the same time.

Having been given a task, all four students respond at the same time – answering, solving, adding, developing, drawing or whatever the task demands. Once they have all finished, (or when the teacher signals 'time's up') they swap papers with each other, passing their papers in a clockwise direction and repeat so that each student now adds to the previous student's work. This process continues until the 'round' is complete.

This second variation is perfect for use when you want students to work on related sub-topics. For example, in a science lesson on elements each team member would add to a list of properties for separate elements; in an English lesson each team member could contribute to a separate character profile.

Active/Cooperative Activity #8

Peer Lessons

Overview: There is some truth in the old saying 'You never really learn a subject until you teach it'. In this activity each group is involved in preparing and teaching new information to the rest of the class.

Number of people: Any group size.

Materials: Suitable teaching and resource preparation materials should be made available for students to choose from including poster making materials, visual aids and props.

Time: This activity is designed to last for an entire lesson although additional time (during preceding lessons) needs to be allocated for preparation and research.

Directions:

1. Students are placed in teams of four. Teams can be randomly selected but this activity works best with diverse groupings so that low ability students can be given the motivation and support they may need.

2. Each group is given a topic, skill, concept or piece of information to teach to the rest of the group.

3. Students are given time to research their task and decide how they will present their information (in a preceding lesson). They are encouraged to avoid lecture presentations so as to make the learning experience as active as possible and must make sure all group-members are involved in some capacity in the teaching process.

Suggestions for teaching methods could include:

- Visual aids
- Role-plays/skits

- Quiz games and puzzles
- Q and A sessions
- Puzzles
- Practical sessions
- Production of worksheets, handouts and reading material

4. Each group presents their lesson to the rest of the class

Active/Cooperative Activity #9

Russian Roulette

Overview: Using dice to randomly select turn-taking always injects fun into a task. Students work in groups to answer pre-written questions.

Number of people: Any group size – split into groups of four.

Materials: An ordinary die can be used for this activity – despite the fact that there are only four students in a group – by making the numbers five and six void. When these numbers are rolled, everyone can have a quick rest. Alternatively, use the dice templates in your resource area to create your own dice with suitable 'group forfeits' assigned to the two extra numbers.

http://needsfocusedteaching.com/kindle/active/

Pre-written question cards are also required as described below.

Time: 10-30 minutes depending on the complexity of the questions

This activity can be applied to a wide range of topics in several ways. For example, in any subject, the cards could have a straightforward consolidation or revision question to answer. Alternatively, in social studies or humanities subjects, a topic could be explored and discussed from various angles by assigning each card to a particular character, role or viewpoint.

Another variation is to have students put segments of information in a logical sequence. As students throw the die, they must give the 'next step' in a series. In modern foreign languages the cards could be used to prompt development of a story, sentence by sentence. Each card would have a word, phrase or even picture on it which must be used in the next sentence.

As a simple example, student 'four' throws a 'two'. Student 'two' picks up the first card which has 'Dog' written on it. He/she must then say a sentence with the word 'dog' in it. The next student whose number comes up on the die would then have to continue the story from the first sentence using the word on his/her card.

Directions:

1. Students work in groups of four with each being given a number (one to four). Each group is given a stack of question cards which are placed in the centre of their table.

2. The first player rolls the die and the person with the number shown picks up the top card and responds to the question appropriately.

3. The next plays then rolls the die and, again, the person with the number shown picks up the next card and answers the question. This continues round the circle until all the cards have been used up.

Active/Cooperative Activity #10

Three Stage Fish Bowl

Number of people: Class of around 30-35 is optimum.

Materials: None required.

Time: 30 mins

Directions:

1. Teacher writes three discussion questions relevant to the lesson topic. Ideally the questions should be linked but this isn't totally necessary.

2. Chairs are arranged in concentric circles as for the Fish Bowl exercise with the inner circle of chairs facing the outer circle of chairs.

3. Count students off into 1's, 2's and 3's. Ask the 1's to sit in the inner circle seats and 2's and 3's to sit in the outer circle seats.

4. Teacher asks the first question from the list of three and invites the 1's to give their response to the 2's and 3's (each '1' will be directing his/her answer at two people sitting opposite - a '2' and a '3').

5. Allow 5 minutes for this phase and then ask the 2's to swap seats with the 1's. The teacher reads out the second question. The 2's can now have two minutes to add to the comments made by the 1's before giving their response to the teacher's second question.

6. The procedure is repeated for the 3's

7. When all three questions have been answered, the entire group is reconvened and students share their answers.

Active/Cooperative Activity #11

Terror Cards

Number of people: Particularly useful with large groups

Materials: Index cards – one for each student

Time: N/A

Overview:

Terror cards provide a great way of making sure that all students are included in a lesson. They are particularly beneficial in large groups where individuals may get 'missed' or 'forgotten' during Q & A sessions and other activities. The teacher randomly picks a terror card to identify who will participate in a given activity.

Directions:

1. Have students write their first name and initial on an index card.

2. Teacher shuffles the deck of cards and stores them in a box on his/her desk.

3. Whenever a response is required from a student a Terror Card is drawn from the deck and the named student is called on to answer/participate.

4. The card is returned to the box of cards.

Active/Cooperative Activity #12

Relay

Number of people: 10-30

Materials: 10 Pre-written question cards on coloured cards for each group – a different colour for each group

Time: 20-30 mins

Overview:

This is an activity which gets students up on their feet – great for kinesthetic learners. It also promotes group cohesion as team members work together to solve problems.

Directions:

1. Students form diverse groups of three or four.

2. Each group is assigned a colour and a pile of question cards for each group is placed on the teacher's desk with question one on the top (blue cards for blue group etc.)

3. Each group is provided with resource materials – reference books, handouts etc. Ideally there should be materials for each team member to make sure everyone is involved.

4. Each group assigns a 'runner'. The 'runner' runs to the front and grabs their team's first question and takes it back to their group. The group then works together to find the answer from the resource materials and a 'scribe' writes the team's answer on an answer sheet. When they think they have the correct answer a new 'runner' takes their answer to the front and the teacher checks it to make sure it is correct.

5. If their answer is correct the same runner takes question card two from their team's pile and returns to the group to find an answer. If their answer is incorrect the teacher sends them back to try again.

When the 'runner' is at the teacher's desk the rest of the team members read through the reference materials to prepare for the next question.

6. The first team to get through all the questions wins a prize (shown to students beforehand to encourage them to work harder). At the end the teacher hands out model answers to the group for revision purposes.

NB/ Make the first few questions easy to get the activity off to a good start and make sure students have a clear route to the front desk to minimize chances of tripping or falling.

Active/Cooperative Activity #13

Four Musketeers

Number of people: Of particular use with large groups

Materials: Pre-written questions. (Questions which promote discussion or require more than a 'one word answer' are most suited to this activity). Terror Cards for students (see above)

Time: 10-15 mins per question

Overview:

The motto of the Three Musketeers was 'All for one and one for all.' This activity has a similar principle in that team members work together for the good of the group. It's different in that students form groups of four rather than three.

Directions:

1. Students form groups of four where possible.

2. Teacher reads out a question and gives a few minutes for students to work individually and write an answer down.

3. Teacher gives 'discussion time' for students to discuss their answers with the rest of their group members. Students are encouraged to help each other during this phase so that everyone's answer is improved and everyone has a good understanding.

4. Teacher calls 'time' and draws a 'Terror Card'. The relevant student answers the question using the combined knowledge of his/her team mates.

Active/Cooperative Activity #14

Common Goal Jigsaw

Overview:

A structured way of dealing with questions, encouraging discussion and promoting team work. This is similar to Activity 3 **'Group Learn and Teach'** but in this version, groups of students become 'experts' on one particular topic and then, rather than each tem member simply summarising the information they have learned, they each pool their knowledge with their other group members in order to reach a common goal or complete a group task.

Directions:

1. The teacher divides the whole class into diverse groups of four. Each group should reflect the balance of the whole class in terms of gender, ability and attitude and is known as a **'BASE GROUP'**.

2. Each group is given a common task. Handouts are employed in order to set the task. Reading material is kept to a manageable length and complexity. If the **Base Groups** are of four, then there are four questions or tasks within the main task – one for each member of the group. Questions or tasks are allocated within each group, through negotiation between the students.

3. All the students who have selected a particular question or task now regroup into **Expert Groups** and work together on what is now a common problem and outcome. Each exert group is given suitable research material or relevant tools & resources (if it is a practical task). By the time this stage of the session is completed, each has become an expert on this matter, through discussion and collaboration with the other 'experts'.

4. Original groups reform. Dissemination begins. The Base Groups are set a final task. This could be a group outcome, or an individual task.

The crucial element is to ensure that students have to draw on the combined 'wisdom' of the home group in order to complete the task.

Active/Cooperative Activity #15

Arrows for Understanding

Overview: Using arrows for understanding is a great way to check for student understanding during instruction. Students each hold up a small laminated card with an arrow as you ask them questions during class. The directions in which they point the arrows indicate their answers, so you can easily tell if the class understands the instruction or not. This is also helpful for students who may have problems raising their hands in class if they have questions. If their arrow points the wrong way, you will quickly be able to assess their understanding and correct any misunderstandings, or answer any additional questions they may have.

Number of people: Entire class.

Materials: One small (5" X 8") piece of paper or cardstock, with a large arrow on one side, laminated for durability and future use (see attached template).

Time: During instruction.

Directions:

1. Before instruction starts, pass out a laminated arrow card to each student. Tell students that they will use these arrow cards to indicate their answers to questions that you will pose throughout the lesson.

2. During instruction, ask students to indicate their answers to questions by pointing their arrows in a certain direction. This is especially useful if you are comparing and contrasting two things. Write one answer on the left side of the chalkboard, and the contrasting answer on the right side of the chalkboard. As they

answer, students will be able to point their arrows towards in the correct direction, as you ask them questions.

3. For yes or no questions, instruct students to point their arrows up for "yes" and down for "no."
4. Depending on the questions, students will hold up their arrow cards, which you can easily see, and determine whether they understand the subject correctly, or not. This is a great way to correct any misunderstandings as they occur, keeping the entire class on the right track.
5. Once instruction is over, have students hand back the arrow cards for use in future instruction.

Active/Cooperative Activity #16

Folder Pass

Overview: Folder Pass is a great way to have students review the central problems, questions, or fundamental elements of a lesson. As a group, students will review their knowledge of a topic and compile their answers in each folder, eventually creating a class wide understanding of the topic. This review activity is especially beneficial to shy students, who will work with the members of their group to come up with answers to the question, rather than being singled out in class.

Number of people: Entire class, arranged into 4-6 groups of students.

Materials: Four to six file folders.

Time: 5-15 minutes, depending on class discussion.

Directions:

1. Before the activity, create four to six questions that are central to the lesson. Write each question down on a single paper, and staple each paper inside an empty file folder.

2. Divide students into four to six groups, the same amount of groups as folders, and hand out one folder to each group of students.

3. As a group, students will read the question and come up with an answer, which they will write down in one sentence on the paper in the folder, and then pass the folder to the next group. To make this step easier, set a time limit for each question, and have groups pass folders at the same time.

4. After each group has answered each one of the questions in the folder, go around the class from group to group and have the students in each group read the question and all answers aloud to the class.

5. Initiate a class discussion after each of the folders have been reviewed to ensure accuracy of the answers and to see if any students have anything to add to the answers.

Active/Cooperative Activity #17

Role-Play Strips

Overview: Role Play strips are a great way to begin a new unit, as well as to get students involved and interested in the new subject. In this group exercise, students take on a role assigned to them randomly, and ask and answer questions based on this role. This exercise is designed to get students to see the many sides of a problem, and learn how to use information to help them argue their point, as well as to get them interested in the topic.

Number of people: Entire class, organized into groups of three to four.

Materials: One set of Role Play strips per group of students, timer.

Time: 20-30 minutes.

Directions:

1. Before the exercise begins, prepare a set of role play strips. Decide on three or four different roles within the subject you are teaching. For example, if you are beginning a unit on nuclear energy, one role would be of the nuclear scientist, one role would be of a concerned citizen, and another role would be of a city developer. Don't be afraid to get creative and make the roles as specific as possible. Write down each role separately on a strip of paper, and make as many sets of strips as you will have groups of students. Once you have completed your roles, make a list of questions that each one of the students in the group will have to answer, based on the perspective of the role which they have been assigned. To continue with the nuclear energy example from above, one of your questions would be "Is nuclear energy a safe alternative to traditional forms of energy?" or "Should we use nuclear energy in our city? Why or why not?"

2. When you begin the exercise in class, organize the students into groups of three to four each. Make sure you have enough roles per group so that each student will have their own specific role to play. Randomly assign each student a role strip from the set of role strips. No one in the group should have the same roles.

3. Write your role play questions on the board and instruct each one of the students to write down their answers to the questions, based on the perspective of the role they have been assigned. For example, if the student was assigned the role of the nuclear scientist, he or she would answer the questions based from the perspective of science. Give students one minute to write down their answer, then allow students one or two minutes to quickly discuss each one of their answers within the group. After the first question is done, continue with the rest of the questions as above, until all questions have been answered in the group. Depending on the number of questions, this part of the exercise may take a bit of time. Keep students on track by using a timer or clock to guide them in answering their questions.

To save time, you may only want to ask one very central question, rather than many simple questions.

4. After student groups are done answering all of the questions, lead the class in a discussion about their answers, and how the role-playing exercise helped them to see the many sides of the problem. Use this discussion to lead the class into an in-depth study of the topic or unit.

Grouping Students for Cooperative & Active Learning

Grouping Methods

There are many ways to group students when you're preparing a group activity. Different types of groupings have different benefits and challenges, so the type you choose depends on various factors. In some cases it might be suitable to allow students to pick their own groups but generally it will be up to the teacher to decide which groupings work best for the class and for particular projects. Groupings should be rotated and changed regularly so that the whole class group interacts and doesn't degenerate into cliques.

Grouping Method #1

Random Groups

This is one of the quickest ways to form groups and is best suited to activities where the ability mix of individuals is not so important, such as brainstorming sessions, games and other fun activities, or with new groups of individuals you don't yet know particularly well. Like friendship groups (where students are simply told to get together in a group with their friends), students see this as a 'fair' way to be grouped as it is based on chance rather than a deliberate choice made by the teacher. As you get to know your students you will naturally find that grouping some individuals together is not appropriate, and you will gradually move away from 'random groupings' to more planned and organised methods explained below.

Ideas for forming 'Random Groups'

i) Stick a pen in the register

This is obviously a very quick and easy technique and doesn't really warrant an explanation.

ii) Pull names out of a hat

As above.

iii) Number round the class

Although a very quick and easy way of forming random groups, there is potential for sub-grouping part-way through an activity if necessary with this method; e.g. start by counting the class off in fours – 1, 2, 3, 4... 1, 2, 3, 4... etc. and have each 'group of four' work together for the first activity. Have the class re-group later by putting all the ones together in one group, all the twos together in another group, and so on.

HOT TIP:

If you want your sub-groups to form with minimum disruption and confusion (who wouldn't?), deal with them in stages and get them to identify themselves to each other. Simply telling all the 'ones' to get together will cause chaos because nobody knows who all the 'ones' are – they will be shouting out to each other to try and identify the right group. You can eliminate this problem very easily by giving stepped instructions which help students identify other potential group members - even in a busy, crowded classroom:

"All the 'ones' raise your right hand." ...Pause... "Keep your hand raised until you are in a group of four 'ones'. Once you have found three other number 'ones', put your hands down and sit down in your new group."

Give them a few minutes and then go through the other teams.

iv) Comic strips:

Here's a slightly more creative grouping method... Cut cartoon strips into separate frames – one strip for each group. If you want to form six groups, you need six different cartoon strips – perhaps taking each from one comic. For example, The Beano would provide strips such as Minnie The Minx, Dennis the Menace, Roger the Dodger etc.

The frames from strips are mixed up and one frame is given to each student as they enter the room. They then have to find other members from the same cartoon to form their 'strip'. After the participants have found everyone in their group, they must arrange themselves so that the sequence of frames is in chronological order to form the comic strip correctly - and then sit down together.

v) Colour/shape Cards:

This is another method which is well suited to sub-groupings. Issue each student a colour/shape card. See template in your resources, here:

http://needsfocusedteaching.com/kindle/active/

Four groups can then be formed by choosing one shape and giving each student a card in one of the four colours. i.e. all students would be given a circle card and then split into reds, blues, greens and yellows.

There are further opportunities for group sub-division if the different shapes are also brought in to play. In a class of thirty-two (for ease of explanation), there would be eight teams of four. We could issue eight of each colour card to the class members to get our initial grouping. This would give us two teams of four in each colour.

If we wanted the option of splitting the groups later in the activity, instead of giving cards with one shape as above, we would give out two shape cards for each colour. i.e. the main red group would no longer consist of eight circles but would now be two red triangles, two red squares, two red circles and two red rectangles. We would split this group into two red subgroups each consisting of one of each shape. This is not as complicated as it sounds!

Later in the activity each student could form a new group with three new members by putting all the shapes together instead of the colours.

"OK, we're going to form new groups and share what we've learned. You need to find three new team members who have the same SHAPE as you but in a different colour. In your new group you should have four different coloured versions of your shape."

vi) Puzzles:

Simple jigsaw puzzles can be made by sticking pictures from magazines on to cardboard and then cutting the picture up to your desired shape, size and number of pieces or, of course, they can be bought from toy shops. You want large simple puzzles – the type for very young children if you're buying them – with five or six pieces.

You need the same number of puzzles as groups you're trying to create – i.e. if you want to split the class into six groups of five, you need six puzzles, each with at least five pieces.

Mix up the pieces from all the puzzles and give each student a puzzle piece. When you are ready to form the students into groups, put some music on and instruct them to find others with pieces from their puzzle. The groups should sit down with their completed puzzle in front of them.

HOT TIP:

If you want to get really clever you can source pictures which have a link to the lesson content and use these as prompts for starter questions.

vii) Chocolate Bars:

This method is very popular with students and is nice to use on a special occasion or when you are trying to get a difficult group on side.

Buy a range of chocolate bars or small packets of sweets/candy. Again, you need the same number of sweet types as groups you want to form. The best to use are the 'fun size' chocolate bars – you get around fifteen-twenty of one type in a bag. So if you want six groups of five you need six different types of candy and five of each type.

Stick one chocolate bar/packet of candy under each seat using tape and when you want the students to form their groups ask them to check their seat to find their gift. They then arrange themselves in groups of the same candy type.

To make sure groups don't get mixed up put a large picture of each candy type on the wall in different places around the room. All the 'Mars' bars meet under the 'Mars' picture, all the pastilles meet under the pastille picture etc.

Oops, nearly forgot. Remember to check for food allergies on the SEN register before running this one!

viii) Families:

Create a list of 'famous family members' or cartoon characters in groups of four or five (the number of participants you want in each group). For example: Homer, Marge, Bart, Lisa; Peter Pan, Tinkerbell, Captain Hook, Wendy; Batman, Robin, The Penguin, The Joker etc.

Write each name on a separate piece of card and give each student a name card as they enter the room or when you want to form them into groups. Each student then has to find the other members of their 'family'.

ix) Animals:

This last method is noisy... but it's also excellent fun.

Give each student an 'Animal Card' as they enter the room – you'll find these in your resources, here: http://needsfocusedteaching.com/kindle/active/

NB// you need to produce sufficient cards of each type according to the number of participants you want in each group – if you want five students per group, make sure you make five copies of each animal.

When you want them to form their groups they have to find other team members without speaking or showing their cards. They do so by making the sound of the animal on their card. i.e. all the cows will be 'moo-ing', sheep will be 'baa-ing', donkeys will be 'ee-awing', pigs will be 'oink-ing' etc. Those making the same sound will form a group.

This type of grouping is also ideal for any activity which requires participants to feedback to the rest of the class – such as fun quizzes. The benefit being that when they want to respond to a question they have a ready-made 'buzzer' – their animal sound.

Grouping Method #2

Mixed-Skills Groups

With this grouping method students with DIFFERENT skills or strengths are grouped together. Each group might have, for example, a note-taker with neat hand-writing, a natural leader who acts as motivator, a talented artist, and a confident presenter. Students then naturally fall into a role that benefits their group.

Some teachers like to assign roles within groups, helping students along and sometimes challenging students with roles that they wouldn't necessarily have chosen. As the teacher, you can assign roles by handing out cards for various roles, such as "note-taker," "reporter", "presenter", "motivator," "artist," etc. By handing a specific card to each student in a group, the teacher controls what exactly each student will do. This is a helpful way to approach mixed-skills groups in classrooms that are particularly rowdy, or with students who aren't familiar with group work and wouldn't necessarily know how to assign roles themselves. This grouping helps motivate individuals because everyone has an important part to play in their group's success – it relies on peer encouragement.

Grouping Method #3

Similar-skills groups

With this method students with SIMILAR skills and strengths are grouped together. This is more effective if you are working on a large class project - each small group can then focus on just one aspect of that project. If you are producing a play, for example, you could have a group of artistic students responsible for the scenery; a group of creative and active students responsible for finding costumes; and a group of writers responsible for perfecting the script.

This type of group doesn't work for all projects, since group assignments usually involve various tasks that require different skills. The one major benefit from this type of group, though, is that students get to do what they are good at. This grouping helps motivate individuals because they get to develop (or 'show off') their skills in an area they already enjoy.

Grouping Method #4

Interest Groups

Like similar-skills groups, interest groups only work for certain projects. They are especially effective for research projects, where students who are interested in researching a specific topic can work together. When preparing for this type of group, it helps to have students write down their top 3 choices (of research topics or other topics that will determine their groups) on a card. This works best if you present the topics and have students immediately write down their choices, so they don't get to discuss topics with their friends and agree to write only what their friends are writing.

The students' choices determine their groups (though you may have to intervene if you know that certain groupings won't work – this is one reason why you should have students write several choices on their cards). If, for example, the class has been studying mediaeval Europe, you might end up with one group focusing on knights, one on castles, one on medicine, and one on the daily life of serfs. It is then up to you to decide how you want students to do this research. Are they each going to do their own research, with the group just there to help problem-solve? Or is each group going to present one project, with each member focusing on one aspect of the project? In this case, you may also find it useful to assign individual roles in the group so students can complete the project effectively. This grouping helps motivate individuals because they get to work with, and bounce ideas off, those with similar interests.

Grouping Method #5

Performance Groups

In this type, the teacher groups students together by current levels of performance in a certain subject, so that students who want to move faster can do so with their group, and students who need more time can take that time with a slower group. This is an ideal way for a language-arts teacher to assign various books in a class of widely varying abilities. The teacher can group students by reading ability and then assign appropriate books to each group.

This works best when the teacher also assigns tasks for the group to complete as they read; maybe they have to find five vocabulary words in each chapter, create and answer ten reading questions for each chapter, or design a poster to teach the rest of the class about the book. For younger students, each group could have their own spelling list, so that good spellers can move ahead more quickly than those who struggle with it. This method helps motivate individuals because students get to move at a pace that works for them – faster workers won't get bored while less able students don't get so frustrated or feel left behind.

Grouping Method #6

Support Groups

In this type we group one or two students who are strong in a subject with one or two students who need support in that subject. This type of grouping can cause some students to feel superior and others to feel second class, so you need to be careful how you use this grouping. It often works best when you're not trying to teach an academic concept, but rather a certain skill, such as organisation. Students who are particularly well-organised might get a great deal of satisfaction (whilst developing their social skills) out of helping a perpetually less advanced peer. It's crucial for the teacher in these situations to convey the idea that those needing support are NOT inferior in any way, but simply lacking skills in this one particular area. If teachers can group students in such a way that the ones being supported can also teach their supporters an important skill, these groups will be most effective.

Diverse Groups

This type of grouping maximises potential for peer tutoring, social development and classroom management whilst avoiding cliques which can lead to bullying, refusal to work, lack of social interaction and other classroom management issues. It is this particular type of grouping which has been shown, through various research studies, to show significant gains in academic achievement.

Generally, a diverse group will consist of a high achiever, a low achiever and two middle achievers and the group will ideally consist of males and females. When appropriate, ethnic groups will also be equally represented.

Diverse groups are created for long term projects and whole schemes of work – usually spanning three to six weeks or so. If groups are changed more frequently than this there is insufficient time for individuals to bond as a team and if they are never changed, the opportunities for students to use their social skills in new groupings are lost. Teams should always be changed from time to time, even when team-members are working well together, not just because it gives students the chance to further broaden their communication skills and ability to bond with others but also to give team members a break from each other. Invariably, some teams won't get on as harmoniously as others. Subjecting students to the same groupings indefinitely when they don't get on well is unfair and will be detrimental to their own development as well as creating unnecessary management issues.

Although diverse groups have been shown to stimulate academic achievement this should never be the only grouping type used in cooperative sessions. If it was, the benefits of the other types of groupings would not be realised so from time to time the teacher should use groupings such as random groups, mixed skills, similar skills, interest, performance and support groups to get the most from students and allow them to get the most from each other.

How to Form Diverse Groups

There are several methods for forming diverse groups. None of them are particularly simple and it will take some time to settle on suitable groupings. It is, however, well worth the effort.

The first issue you need to be cautious of is that students should not be aware that they are being grouped according to ability. That means we have to be a bit sneaky when forming the groups.

The two methods I'm going to present first here are pretty low tech but there are also two other methods which will undoubtedly save you time. Regardless of the method you use, you will need the following in order to progress: a class list with students ranked according to their ability level.

To make it simple, we rank ability by three broad groups – Low, Medium and High. The following picture shows what I mean but it doesn't have to be completed in a spreadsheet. You can use paper. Or the back of an old envelope. Or even a beer mat if you're doing this in the pub after work.

Diverse Grouping Method #1

Two Pairs

This method is most popular with students because they have some control over who they choose to group with. The downside is that you can't use it with all groups. If there is a broad range of abilities in the class and students are conscious of this fact, this grouping won't work so well.

Start by using your class list to split the group into four clear groups. Put the 'high' ability students in one corner of the room, the 'low' ability students in another corner and then split the 'medium' ability students into two groups, putting one group in each of the remaining two corners of the room. This obviously assumes you have four corners in your classroom. If you're working in a hexagonal room, adapt as necessary.

Next, ask the students from the high corner to find a partner from ONE of the 'medium' corners. Get students to raise one hand in the air until they find a partner and then put their hands down when they have done so. That way they can immediately see who is available.

Next, ask the 'low' corner students to find a partner from the other 'medium' corner in the same way as above.

The low/medium paired students should now stand on one side of the room facing the high/medium pairs. All that's needed now is for each pair to pair up again with a pair from the opposite side of the room.

This gives groups of four, each with two medium ability students, one high ability and one low ability.

You'll find that if left to their own devices, the students will invariably pick pairs of their own sex. Diverse groups should ideally have an equal number of boys and girls so you might stipulate that partners of a different sex must be picked during the first pairing, and pairs of a different sex must be picked in the second pairing.

Once the teams have been formed make a note of the team members for each group so that in later sessions you can have them form new teams with different members to those they are currently with.

Diverse Grouping Method #2

Post-It© Notes

This method is much easier to orchestrate from the teacher's point of view and provides a really easy way of changing groups around if they're not working. It also provides a handy visual reference for students.

Using your ability-ranked class list write the name of each student on a colour-coded Post-It© Note/sticky note. Remember that the medium ability students will be sub-divided into two groups so that you will have four groups in total – 'medium' on one colour note, 'high' on another and the two 'low' groups each on two different coloured notes.

Groups can now be selected by taking one student from each colour group and putting them together on a team sheet (a large piece of paper or card). Individuals can easily be moved from group to group until a satisfactory grouping is obtained thanks to the wonderful re-stickable properties of the Post-It Note® and the finished team sheet can then be put on display for easy reference.

HOT TIP:

Some students just love to mess teachers around by changing the arrangement of the notes to cause confusion. You can prevent that by coating the sheet with some clear polythene.

A note on gender:

Of course it may not always be possible to have an equal ratio of boys to girls on each team - but wherever possible do try to avoid having one boy with three girls, or vice versa. This grouping usually results in the boy or girl in question either being totally ignored or, if the gene pool has been kind to them, being given undue attention. It is better to have two of each sex on as many teams as possible and then, if necessary, have a team all of the same sex for the remainders.

Diverse Grouping Method #3

Spreadsheet Method

The students' names are added to a spreadsheet to create a class list in general order of ability. In the diagram below, high ability students are black, middle ability students are dark blue and low ability students are light blue. Note that this is a very general ranking in terms of ability – it doesn't have to be perfect. The ranking can be based on past work, test scores, teacher observation etc.

Select a team by taking a student from the top of the list (high ability student), a student from the bottom of the list (a low ability student) and two students from the middle group (middle ability students) and place them in a team of four. Continue in this way until all students have been placed in a mixed ability team.

Students can be allocated to teams in this way unless they are all the same sex or are likely to cause problems when placed together due to all being silly, talkative or worst enemies.

Groups where all members are of the same character types should also be avoided – a group of introverts will be as incompatible as a group of students who all like being in charge.

Once you have selected TEAM 1, highlight the respective students' names on the main class list so you know they have already been allocated to a team. You can then put the remaining names into the other teams, highlighting names on the class list as they are used up.

Continue allocating students in this way until all students have been placed in a team. If you have an 'extra' student, assign them to make a team of five. Where there are two 'extras' create two teams of three using one of the students from a team of four.

The spreadsheet should be saved with the appropriate title added to give a record of the teams. This will enable you to try new teams for future assignments by having a clear record of who has already worked together.

Diverse Grouping Method #4

Team Maker Software

Team Maker™ software is the AUTOMATIC way to group your students into cooperative learning teams – it makes creating diverse groups from your class list an absolute cinch. You simply type the students' names into the database and Team Maker™ sorts the students into multiple table groups according to their ability level and gender in a ready-to-print group list.

If you aren't happy with a grouping you can then manually fine tune it by moving students from one table group to another or simply press 'shuffle' to get Team Maker™ to create an entirely new grouping automatically.

A copy of Team Maker is available free in the resource area here:

http://needsfocusedteaching.com/kindle/active/

Managing Active Group Work Sessions

We can't just put students into groups and expect the session to run along smoothly – it takes careful management to run a successful session.

This section is about managing group work sessions so that problems are, as much as is possible, prevented from happening. Obviously, the more effectively we pre-empt and prevent problems, the more pleasant the session will be.

The first step in preventing problems is to make sure all students know exactly what they will be doing during the session. In our classroom management courses we use the analogy of giving them a clear map to follow so that there is more chance of them getting where you want them to go.

This means giving very clear, step by step instructions which prevent misinterpretation as far as possible. Steer clear from words such as 'appropriately', 'properly' and 'quietly'. These are abstract terms and mean different things to different individuals. When our instructions are open to misinterpretation we open the door to arguments...

Teacher: *"Work quietly"*

Student: *"I am working quietly!"*

See what I mean? Unless we stipulate exactly what is meant by the word 'quietly', we are going to get students working at different noise levels and each of them can then, quite legitimately, argue that they are working quietly. Definite phrases and precise instructions leave no room for such arguments.

A definite phrase, for example, could be "Work in silence". There is no argument with this – there are no degrees of 'silence'. You are either being silent or you're not. Definite phrases cut out the opportunities for students to argue their point. A student can't say "I was being silent" if they were making a noise.

If that's too draconian for you, use **precise instructions** instead. A precise instruction could be "Work at noise level two" (assuming you are displaying a noise level meter in the room) or "Use your 'Partner Voices'" (having first explained to students what you mean by 'partner voices' together with the acceptable noise level when using them).

Here's another simple example of how precise instructions cut out arguments. Which set of instructions is likely to get the desired result?

A) Teacher: *"Get on with your work please"*

B) Teacher: *"Ryan, you need to finish drawing the diagram and get it labeled in the next ten minutes. After that, answer questions 1-4 underneath your diagram. OK? Now tell me what I just asked you to do please."*

Can you see how Teacher B prevents the common responses such as *"I didn't understand"* or *"I didn't hear you"*?

Did you also notice that she also asks Ryan to repeat her instructions? This cuts out the need for Ryan to say *"I didn't understand what you wanted me to do"* or *"I didn't hear you"* - one less problem to deal with.

Use precise instructions to explain to students the objectives of the task, the procedure to complete it and materials to use.

The second step in Preventing Problems in group work sessions (or any classroom activity for that matter) is to 'teach' the behaviour that you want to see.

When I run coaching and training sessions at schools I'm amazed at the number of teachers who wait for something to go wrong in the classroom before doing anything about it. This is backward. Instead of waiting for students to get it wrong, why not SHOW (ie 'teach') them what you want them to do SO THAT THEY DON'T GET IT WRONG? (Or at least provide them with as much chance as possible of getting it right).

If you have a student who continually fails to hand homework in when it is due, is there any point in continually waiting for them to do so and then punishing them when they don't? There is a reason why the homework isn't being done and if we can address the reason there is perhaps more chance that the task will be completed in future. We can't always address the reasons for behaviour – many are outside our control but sometimes the extra support shown to a student who is facing outside pressures is enough to encourage them to make positive changes. So a better way, for example, than continual punishment to deal with a student who 'forgets' to do their homework would be to teach them some time-management skills.

There are three main ways to teach your students how you want them to behave during group work...

1. Establish routines

2. Explain & model desired actions

3. Assign student roles

1. Establishing Routines

I'm often asked by teachers how they can become more consistent.

Consistency is a hot topic and the best way I've found to create instant consistency is through the use of routines. A routine cements your instructions in place so that they are the same every time. This means your students develop the right habits through repetition. It is when we give different instructions for a task that we get inconsistencies – and it is difficult for a student to know what to do when the rules or instructions keep changing.

For group work, you need to think about what you want your students to do and how you want them to behave during the group work session. Think about 'hot spots' and problem areas - issues which always tend to create problems, such as asking for help or wandering round the room aimlessly bumping into things. These problems need to be pre-empted and prevented by writing them into your routine – as in the following sample routine.

Sample Routine for Group Work

- Stay in your allotted group

- Ask your team members for help if you have a question

- Help your team mates if you are asked for help

- Ask for help from the teacher only when the group agrees on the same question

- Work within stated noise levels

Once you've decided on a routine it needs to be taught to students, the same way you would introduce and teach any new topic. Demonstrate what you want students to do at each stage of the routine and exactly how you want them to act. Then have them practise this several times over the next few sessions until the routine becomes a habit. Have the routine laminated and displayed on the wall for reference.

You will probably find there are steps within the routine which could become routines in themselves - such as the steps to take to 'ask for help' in the correct manner. If you want your students to ask for help in a certain way, they need to be shown or taught the specific way. A routine needs to be created.

Routines really can automate your classroom and any change to your normal teaching can be made much easier for everyone by turning it into a routine.

2. Explaining & Modelling Acceptable Behaviour

Group work is the perfect medium for reinforcing social skills – in any group work session, students naturally have to interact with each other. In order to cut out problems and ensure they interact in an acceptable manner, key social skills need to be explained and modelled prior to the session. Remember – it's all about giving them a clear map to follow.

The following social skills should be demonstrated/explained prior to, and continually modelled during group work sessions.

Listening skills – explain how you want students to listen to each other.

Remaining calm when others do something you don't agree with– group work naturally promotes discussions which can become heated at times. Students therefore need to be shown how to keep their tempers and remain calm (we'll assume you have frisked them for weapons before class began).

Helping when someone is struggling & encouraging team spirit – learning to act as a team player is something which doesn't come naturally to some students. It needs to be explained and taught.

3. Assigning roles

The reason some students do nothing during group work and others lazily copy from other students is that they do not have specific tasks or jobs to complete during the session. By assigning student roles you give accountability – students are involved from the start of the task.

For instance, in a group of four:

Student 1 could be responsible for materials - collecting the materials/resources and returning them to the appropriate place when the day or period is over; making sure none get lost (materials, not students) and that damages are reported to the teacher.

Student 2 could be responsible for seeing that the steps of the activity are followed.

Student 3 could be responsible for making observations, recording data, and taking minutes as the activity progresses.

Student 4 could be responsible for overseeing the writing of the group report.

Other roles might include:

Quality controller – checks other students' work and corrects mistakes.

Mr/Mrs Motivator - encourages team members to participate when enthusiasm is waning.

Presenter - feeds back to the rest of the class by way of individual or group presentation.

Assigning roles can be done by the teacher or the students themselves. Where student strengths and weaknesses are particularly pronounced, the teacher should assign roles.

What to do when some students won't do their share of the work in a group

This is a common problem but your first response should NOT be to jump in and solve the problem. Whenever possible, students should be given the opportunity to solve these problems themselves and develop social skills. Solving conflicts such as this proactively and appropriately is a very valuable skill for team members to learn. Your role is to be on hand and help the group when they struggle to solve the problem themselves.

- Talk to other members of the group and encourage them to help each other.

- Encourage group members to offer support to the student who isn't working and make sure he/she fully understands what they are expected to do.

- Encourage group members to suggest an achievable work target for their team mate.

- Show them any episode of The A-Team (last resort only).

If the student is still refusing to work:

- Take them aside and explain that they may have to be taken off group work if they can't stick to the rules.

- Withdraw the student and give them individual work to do.

Managing Noise Levels During Active Sessions

Here are some tips for managing noise levels during group work:

1. Assign a 'noise monitor' to each group

It's their job to keep noise levels at a previously agreed level.

2. Make sure each group has a clearly defined area to work in

Groups should be discouraged from mixing with each other.

3. Use the traffic light system

A green card on the board means noise levels are fine as they are. Orange is a warning that it's getting too rowdy in the room and they need to be quieter. Red is a call for a period of total silence for a while.

4. Use the token system

Give each student three cards or tokens of some sort. Whenever they speak out of turn they have to surrender one of their tokens. If they behave/participate particularly well they can win back tokens.

5. Hands up

Explain that when you have your hand in the air they have to do the same in total silence. The last person to do so gets a check on the board or some other type of small sanction. If they put their hand up but carry on talking it is twice as ignorant so they receive two checks.

6. Sin Bin

Students who aren't buying in to the group session and are spoiling it for the rest of their team are given a clear choice: unless you are prepared to follow the instructions for group work then you will have to work on your own. The 'sin bin' area should be a table well away from other groups with individual tasks prepared and laid out for them to get on with. Be careful not to have more than one student in this area at a time – otherwise the 'sin bin' will be perceived as more fun than the group work session. Have multiple isolated 'sin bins' if necessary.

Ten Extra Tips For Successful Group Work Sessions

1. Set deadlines for tasks. Make sure students are fully aware of time constraints throughout the session with frequent reminders.

"You have twenty minutes left... you should have finished part one by now."

2. Keep tasks achievable and fairly short especially in early sessions – tasks that are too difficult or that go on for too long will cause students to lose interest in future group work sessions.

3. Give each group member a clear role and make sure they understand what this role entails.

4. Have a feedback session at the end of all group work to enable students to discuss what worked well and what didn't.

5. Take photos of students engaged in group work and display them – it is good for students to see themselves having fun.

6. Get groups to come up with a 'team name' before starting work. This adds to the camaraderie and offers more potential for inter-group competition.

7. Have prizes, certificates, stickers, cups, trophies and silly awards – toys etc. which are awarded to students for peak performance in their respective roles.

8. Have an exciting award ceremony at the end of each project where team efforts as well as individual efforts are recognised.

"Best motivator this week is..."

"Best presenter this week is..."

"Special award for someone who resolved conflict between two team members..."

Make the presentations fun and build ceremony into the whole issue of group work.

9. Assign the role of 'reporter' to each team – their task is to write a brief summary of any successes the team members had throughout the project.

10. Always have ten items in your lists – it's a nice round number!

And Finally!

"It made my naughtiest student as quiet as a mouse!"

"Thank you so much for the superbly wonderful videos! I benefited a lot from your creative secret agent method! It made my naughtiest student as quiet as a mouse! THANK YOU..."

Yasaman Shafiee (Take Control of the Noisy Class customer)

Take Control of The Noisy Class

To get your copy, go here:

https://www.amazon.co.uk/Take-Control-Noisy-Class-Super-effective/dp/1785830082/

Also, if you'd like to receive my FREE **Behaviour Tips** on an inconsistent and irregular basis via my email service, just sign up for your free book resources and you'll start receiving my Behaviour Tips.

http://needsfocusedteaching.com/kindle/active/

These contain short, practical ideas and strategies for responding to all kinds of inappropriate classroom behaviour, as well as some handy teaching tips and ideas for improving student engagement. All this will be sent direct to your email inbox once or twice a week, along with occasional notifications about some of our other products, special offers etc.

Obviously, you can opt out of this service any time you wish but in our experience, most people pick up a lot of *wonderful* ideas from these emails. And feel free to forward the messages and resources on to other teachers (staff meetings, staff room, pop them into your Christmas cards etc.).

Just remember to look out for emails from '***Needs Focused Teaching***' so that you don't miss all the goodies.

"Thanks a million. As a fresh teacher, I find this invaluable."

"Finally something concrete and applicable in real life – I've had enough of the people who have never set their foot in a real classroom but know how everything should be done in theory. Thanks a million. As a fresh teacher, I find this invaluable."

Jasna (Take Control of the Noisy Class customer)

Final Reminder!

If you haven't already done so, head on over to the FREE resources page:

http://needsfocusedteaching.com/kindle/active/

One more thing... Please help me get this book to as many teachers as possible, by leaving an honest review...

"I have seen nothing short of miracles occur."

"I have seen nothing short of miracles occur. My students' attitudes and behaviours have improved; they are excited and personally involved in their educational experience! What more could I ask? My E books have become my bible!!! I truly am a disciple!!!!! Love you guys."

Dawn (NeedsFocusedTeaching customer)

Review Request

If you enjoyed this book, please leave me an honest review! Your support really does matter and it really does make a difference. I do read all the reviews so I can get your feedback and I do make changes as a result of that feedback.

If you'd like to leave a review, then all you need to do is go to the review section on the book's Amazon page. You'll see a big button that states "Write a customer review". Click on that and you're good to go!

You can also use the following links to locate the book on Amazon:

https://www.amazon.co.uk/dp/B0742DS5FS

https://www.amazon.com/dp/B0742DS5FS

For all other countries, please head over to the relevant Amazon site and either search for the book title or simply copy and paste the following code in the Amazon search bar to be taken directly to the book:

B0742DS5FS

Have fun and thanks for your support…

Rob

"...your strategies work wonders!"

"Thank you so much Rob for what you are doing for the profession, your strategies work wonders! I have never tried the 'pen' but will do next time! Seriously speaking, I give the link to your productions to many young teachers I know because they are so unhappy sometimes and they need help which they find with what you do! So, thanks again and carry on with your good job!"

Marie (Take Control of the Noisy Class customer)

Suggested resource providers

Name: HowtoLearn.com and HowtoLearn.teachable.com

Specialty: Personalized Learning Assessments, Learning Solutions, Courses for Teachers, Parents and Students.

Website: www.HowtoLearn.com

Details: Online since 1996, the brainchild of best-selling author and college professor, Pat Wyman, known as America's Most Trusted Learning Expert. We invite you to become part of our global community and closed Facebook group. Your Learning Questions Answered at http://www.HowtoLearn.com/your-learning-questions-answered.

Resources: Take our Free Learning Styles Quiz at HowtoLearn.com and check out parent/teacher tested and approved courses at HowtoLearn.teachable.com.

* * *

Name: Time Savers for Teachers (Stevan Krajnjan)

Speciality: Resources guaranteed to save you time.

Website: http://www.timesaversforteachers.com/ashop/affiliate.php?id=7

Details: Popular forms, printable and interactive teacher resources that save time. Stevan Krajnjan was presented with an Exceptional Teacher Award by The Learning Disabilities Association of Mississauga and North Peel in recognition for outstanding work with children who have learning disabilities.

Resources: www.timesaversforteachers.com

* * *

Name: Nicola Morgan (NSM Training & Consultancy).

Speciality: Innovative resources to motivate staff and empower schools.

Website: www.nsmtc.co.uk

Details: NSM Training & Consultancy provides high quality training for teaching/non teaching staff in the UK and internationally. We provide a large range of courses, expert consultancy and guidance, publications, conferences as well as innovative resources to motivate staff and empower schools.

Resources: http://www.nsmtc.co.uk/resources/

* * *

Name: Susan Fitzell

Speciality: Special Education Needs

Website: www.SusanFitzell.com

Details: Seminar Handouts and supplemental resources for Differentiated Instruction, Motivation, Special Education Needs, Co-teaching, and more.

Resources: http://downloads.susanfitzell.com/

* * *

Name: Patricia Hensley

Speciality: Special Education

Website: http://successfulteaching.net

Details: Strategies and ideas for all grade levels. Great resource for new and struggling teachers.

Resources: Free Student Job Description. https://successfulteaching.blogspot.com/2007/10/student-job-description.html

* * *

Name: Julia G. Thompson

Speciality: Educational consultant, writer, and presenter.

Website: www.juliagthompson.com.

Details: Author of The First-Year Teacher's Survival Guide, Julia G Thompson specializes in assisting new teachers learn to thrive in their new profession.

Resources: For 57 free forms and templates to make your school year easier, just click go to her website and click on the Professional Binder page

* * *

Name: Steve Reifman

Speciality: Teaching the Whole Child (Empowering Classroom Management & Improving Student Learning)

Website: www.stevereifman.com

Details: National Board Certified Elementary Teacher & Amazon Best-Selling Author.

Author of '10 Steps to Empowering Classroom Management: Build a Productive, Cooperative Culture Without Using Rewards'

Resources: https://www.youtube.com/user/sreifman (FREE, 1-2 minute videos with tips for teachers & parents)

* * *

Name: Dave Vizard

Speciality: Behaviour Management

Website: www.behavioursolutions.com

Details: Creator of Brain Break materials and Ways to Manage Challenging Behaviour ebook.

Resources: www.behavioursolutions.myshopify.com/pages/brain-breaks

* * *

Name: Marjan Glavac

Specialty: Tips on getting a teaching job (resume, cover letter, interviews); classroom management strategies.

Website: www.thebusyeducator.com

Details: Marjan Glavac is a best selling motivational author, engaging speaker and elementary classroom teacher with over 29 years of teaching experience.

Resources: Free weekly newsletter, 4 free eBooks (http://thebusyeducator.com/homepage.htm)

* * *

Name: Dr. Rich Allen

Specialty: Workshops and keynotes on engagement strategies for students of all ages

Website: greenlighteducation.net

Details: Author of 'Green Light Teaching' and 'The Rock 'n Roll Classroom'

Resources: Please join our Teaching tips community and access lots of free resources and ideas for your classroom by clicking HERE.

* * *

Name: Ross Morrison McGill

Speciality: Managing director at TeacherToolkit Ltd.

Website: https://www.teachertoolkit.co.uk/

Details: Ross Morrison McGill is a deputy headteacher working in an inner-city school in North London. He is the Most Followed Teacher on Twitter in the UK and writes the Most Influential Blog on Education in the UK.

Resources: https://www.amazon.co.uk/Ross-Morrison-McGill/e/B00G33GTEO/ref=dp_byline_cont_book_1

What people say about us

"Even if you have never had "the class from hell", there is something here for you"

"As a PGCE student it is great to have the opportunity to pick up user-friendly and easily accessible information. The 'Behaviour Needs' course provides exactly that. In a series of amusing, creative, fast-paced sections, Rob Plevin builds up a staggering amount of practical and thought provoking material on classroom behaviour management. All of which are easily translated back in the classroom. Even if you have never had "the class from hell", there is something here for you and the follow up information from the website is laden with golden nuggets which will give you loads more ideas and interventions."

Steve Edwards (Workshop Attendee and Take Control of the Noisy Class customer)

* * *

"I want you to know that you have changed the lives of 40 of my students."

"What an informative day. The sessions on positive reinforcement and the importance of relationships were particularly memorable. I want you to know that you have changed the lives of 40 of my students. Thank you!"

Joanne W. (Singapore Workshop Attendee)

* * *

"...We will be inviting Rob back on every possible occasion to work with all of our participants and trainees."

"We were delighted to be able to get Rob Plevin in to work with our Teach First participants. From the start his dynamic approach captivated the group and they were enthralled throughout. Rob covered crucial issues relating to behaviour management thoroughly and worked wonders in addressing the participants' concerns about teaching in some of the most challenging schools in the country. We will be inviting Rob back on every possible occasion to work with all of our participants and trainees."

Terry Hudson, (Regional Director 'Teach First', Sheffield Hallam University)

* * *

"Thank you for helping me to be in more control."

"Rob, thank you very much for sharing your experience and reminding of these simple but effective things to do. Students' behaviour (or actually my inability to control it) is so frustrating that at times it feels that nothing can help. Thank you for helping me to be in more control."

Natasha Grydasova (Take Control of the Noisy Class customer)

* * *

"I am HAPPILY spending my Sat afternoon listening, watching and reading all your extremely helpful information!"

"Thank You Rob! What a wealth of excellent ideas! This is my 30th year teaching! You would think after 30 years teaching that I wouldn't need to be viewing your awesome videos and reading your helpful blog and website. However, I am HAPPILY spending my Sat afternoon listening, watching and reading all your extremely helpful information! Thank You So Much! I will be one of your biggest fans from now on!"

Kelly Turk (Needs Focused Video Pack customer)

* * *

"...terrific for those teachers who are frustrated."

"Great easy-to-listen-to video tips that will be terrific for those teachers who are frustrated. I'm forwarding this email on to the principals in my district right away!"

Sumner price (Take Control of the Noisy Class customer)

* * *

"Many thanks for all these really helpful life-savers!"

"Very many thanks. I have given myself trouble by letting kids into the room in a restless state with inevitable waste of teaching time. Your advice on calming them down in a positive, non-confrontational way and building rapport is very timely. Many thanks for all these really helpful life-savers!"

Philip Rozario (Take Control of the Noisy Class customer)

* * *

"Fantastic way to create a calm and secure learning environment for all the students."

"Thanks so much Rob. Fantastic way to create a calm and secure learning environment for all the students. It's great how you model the way we should interact with the students – firmly but always with respect."

Marion (Take Control of the Noisy Class customer)

* * *

"I will be recommending that the teachers in training that I deal with should have a look at these videos."

These tips and hints are put in a really clear, accessible fashion. As coordinator of student teachers in my school, I will be recommending that the teachers in training that I deal with should have a look at these videos.

Deb (Take Control of the Noisy Class customer)

* * *

"I found Rob Plevin's workshop just in time to save me from giving up."

"I found Rob Plevin's workshop just in time to save me from giving up. It should be compulsory – everybody in teaching should attend a Needs-Focused workshop and meet the man with such a big heart who will make you see the important part you can play in the lives of your most difficult students."

Heather Beames (Workshop Attendee)

* * *

"...the ideas, strategies and routines shared with our teachers have led to improved classroom practice."

"The Needs Focused Behaviour Management workshops in support of teacher training in Northern Ireland have been very well received and the ideas, strategies and routines shared with our teachers have led to improved classroom practice. This has been validated by both inspections at the University and observations of teachers."

Celia O'Hagan, (PGCE Course Leader, School of Education, University of Ulster)

* * *

"I have never enjoyed a course, nor learnt as much as I did with Rob."

"What a wonderfully insightful, non-patronising, entertainingly informative day. I have never enjoyed a course, nor learnt as much as I did with Rob. I was so impressed that I am recommending our school invite Rob along to present to all the staff so that we can all benefit from his knowledge, experience and humour."

Richard Lawson-Ellis (Workshop Attendee)

* * *

"...since I started following the principles in your materials, I have seen a vast improvement."

"Hi Rob, I would just like to say that since I started following the principles in your materials, I have seen a vast improvement. I had to teach a one hour interview lesson yesterday and was told that they thought the lesson was super and they loved my enthusiasm! I got the job!

Diane Greene (Take Control of the Noisy Class customer)

* * *

> *"Thanks to you, students from 30 some schools are truly engaged and not throwing pencils at the sub!"*

Rob, Your student engagement series has been out of this world. I've already used various techniques as a substitute and students said I was **the best sub ever.** Thanks to you, students from 30 some schools are truly engaged and not throwing pencils at the sub!"

Leslie Mueller (Student Engagement Formula customer)

* * *

> *"So often professional development training is a waste of time; you may get one little gem from a whole day of training. You've given numerous strategies in 5 minutes."*

Wow! So many people have gained so much from your videos! Teachers are time poor. A quick grab of effective ideas is what we all need. So often professional development training is a waste of time; you may get one little gem from a whole day of training. You've given numerous strategies in 5 minutes. Thanks for your generosity.

Mary – Ann (Take Control of the Noisy Class customer)

Strategies List

Mini Reviews 12
Active Reviews..12
Reflective Reviews..14
Paired Reviews 14
Picture Reviews 15
Teach-Backs 16
Ready, Steady... TEACH! 16
Group Teach-Back 17
Case Studies 18
Posters 19
Random Teach-back 19
Student Involvers 21
FOCUS CARDS 22
MANTRAS...23
FUN ROUTINES..24
Okay! 25
Sir, Yes Sir!...26
Golf Claps 27
Are you listening?..27
Yahoo/Yaboo 28
Pair Work 29
Peer Teach..29
Task Tennis...30
Test Each Other 30
Develop Questions...31
Re-Cap 31

Reading to Each Other 31
Find a Learning Partner 31
Hands Up (good for older students) 32
Couples Cards 32
Cooperative Group Work 34
Who Knows? 35
Group Learn & Teach 36
Pick a Card, Any Card 39
First Aid 40
Speed Dating 41
Carousel 43
The Round Table 44
Peer Lessons 46
Russian Roulette 47
Three Stage Fish Bowl 48
Terror Cards 49
Relay 50
Four Musketeers 52
Common Goal Jigsaw 53
Arrows for Understanding 54
Folder Pass 55
Role-Play Strips 56
Grouping Methods 59
Random Groups 59
Mixed-Skills Groups 64
Similar-skills groups 65
Interest Groups 65
Performance Groups 66
Support Groups 67

Diverse Groups..**67**
Two Pairs 69
Post-It© Notes..70
Spreadsheet Method...71
Team Maker Software...72

Made in the USA
San Bernardino, CA
02 August 2018